The Wild World of Animals

Leopards

Spotted Hunters

by Lola M. Schaefer

Consultants:
Tammy Quist and Gena St. John
President and Vice President
Society for Wild Cat Education

Bridgestone Books
an imprint of Capstone Press
Mankato, Minnesota

Bridgestone Books are published by Capstone Press
151 Good Counsel Drive, P.O. Box 669, Mankato, Minnesota 56002
http://www.capstone-press.com

Library of Congress Cataloging-in-Publication Data
Schaefer, Lola M., 1950–
    Leopards: spotted hunters/by Lola M. Schaefer.
    p. cm.—(The wild world of animals)
    Includes bibliographical references (p. 24) and index.
    ISBN 0-7368-0966-X
    1. Leopard—Juvenile literature. [1. Leopard.] I. Title. II. Series.
QL737.C23 S286 2002
599.75′54—dc21   00-012548

Summary: An introduction to leopards describing their physical characteristics, habitat, young, food, predators, and relationship to people.

Editorial Credits
Erika Mikkelson, editor; Karen Risch, product planning editor; Linda Clavel, cover designer
    and illustrator; Heidi Schoof, photo researcher

Photo Credits
Cheryl A. Ertelt, 4, 6, 16
Digital Stock, cover
Index Stock Imagery/Lynn Stone, 18
PhotoDisc, Inc., 1
Photo Network/Mark Newman, 8, 10, 12
Tom & Pat Leeson, 20
Visuals Unlimited/Fritz Polking, 14

1 2 3 4 5 6 07 06 05 04 03 02

Table of Contents

Leopards

Leopards are large, wild cats. They have a large head, strong jaws, and sharp claws. Leopards are 5 to 8 feet (1.5 to 2.4 meters) long. They weigh 60 to 200 pounds (27 to 91 kilograms).

A leopard's spots help it blend in with its surroundings. This blending is called camouflage. Animals with camouflage cannot be seen easily in tall grasses, bushes, and trees.

Leopards Are Mammals

Leopards are mammals. Mammals are warm-blooded animals with a backbone. Their body heat stays the same at all temperatures. Mammals are covered with hair or fur. Leopards have short, sleek fur. All leopards have spots on their fur.

sleek
smooth and shiny

A Leopard's Habitat

Leopards live in Africa and Asia. A spotted leopard's habitat is in leaves and grasses. Black panthers hide in thick forests in Africa and Asia. Black panthers are leopards with black spots and black fur.

habitat
the place where
an animal lives

What Do Leopards Eat?

Leopards are carnivores. They eat only meat. Leopards hunt and kill other animals for food. They eat deer, birds, zebras, and gazelles. A large animal will feed a leopard for one week.

Leopards growl, hiss, snarl, grunt, or purr to send messages to each other. Mothers call to their cubs with loud, short purrs. Young leopards meow when they need help.

Mating and Birth

Male and female leopards mate to produce young leopards. Young leopards grow inside their mother for three to four months before birth. Leopards give birth to two to three cubs at a time.

mate

to join together to produce young

Leopard Cubs

Young leopards are cubs. They weigh about one pound (.5 kilogram) at birth. Cubs start eating meat when they are about 3 months old. Cubs must learn how to hunt. They stalk and catch mice and rabbits at first. Cubs later learn to catch larger prey such as deer.

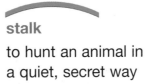

stalk

to hunt an animal in a quiet, secret way

Great Climbers

Leopards use their sharp claws to climb trees. Leopards often hold their prey in their mouth and carry it up a tree. The leopard's food then is safe from other animals. Mother leopards carry their cubs up trees to protect them from enemies.

prey
an animal that is hunted
by another animal for food

Predators

Leopards have many predators. Lions, hyenas, baboons, pythons, and wild dogs eat leopards. Leopards protect themselves by scratching their predators with their sharp claws. Leopards also bite predators with their sharp teeth.

predator

an animal that hunts and eats other animals

Leopards and People

People are a threat to leopards. Hunters often kill leopards for their fur. People are taking over leopards' habitats. Some people want to save leopards living in the wild. Some people build parks where the leopards can live safely.

Hands On: One-of-a-kind Spots

Every leopard has its own pattern of dark spots. See how many different patterns you can create on the face of a leopard using 20 spots.

What You Need

Pencil
White paper
Scissors
Yellow construction paper
Black marker

What You Do

1. Trace the shape shown above onto white paper. Cut out the shape.
2. Trace the shape 10 times onto the yellow construction paper.
3. Cut out the 10 shapes.
4. Use the black marker to make a pattern of 20 spots on one of the leopard faces you cut out.
5. Make a different pattern using 20 dark spots on each of the other shapes.
6. Can you see a difference between your patterns?
7. Could you make more patterns with the spots?

Words to Know

carnivore (KAR-nuh-vor)—an animal that eats only meat

mammal (MAM-uhl)—a warm-blooded animal that has a backbone; female mammals feed milk to their young.

mate (MATE)—to join together to produce young; male and female leopards mate to produce cubs.

predator (PRED-uh-tur)—an animal that hunts and eats other animals

stalk (STAWK)—to hunt an animal in a quiet, secret way

warm-blooded (warm-BLUHD-id)—having a body temperature that stays the same

Read More

McDonald, Mary Ann. *Leopards.* Chanhassen, Minn.: Child's World, 2001.

St. Pierre, Stephanie. *Leopards.* In the Wild. Chicago: Heinemann Library, 2001.

Internet Sites

The CATalog
http://www.wildcateducation.org/catalog/catalog.html
Cyber Zoomobile: Leopard
http://www.primenet.com/~brendel/leopard.html
Leopard
http://ds.dial.pipex.com/agarman/leopard.htm

Index

599.75   Schaefer, Lola M., 1950-
Sch   Leopards : spotted
            hunters

SEP 3 0 2008		
FEB 1 1		
SEP 2 1 2012		
NOV 1 5 2012		
JAN 2 5 2013		
JAN - 6 2014		

Demco, Inc. 38-293

F+P-M

AR 2.8
05 pB